To: ___DADDY_____

From: _____

Other books by Gregory E. Lang:

Why a Daughter Needs a Dad

Why a Daughter Needs a Mom

Why a Son Needs a Mom

Why I Love Grandma

Why I Love Grandpa

Why I Chose You

Why I Love You

Why I Still Love You

Why I Need You

Why We Are a Family

Why We Are Friends

Brothers and Sisters

Sisters

Simple Acts

Love Signs

Life Maps

Thank You, Mom

Thank You, Dad

Why a Son Needs a Dad

· 100 Reasons ·

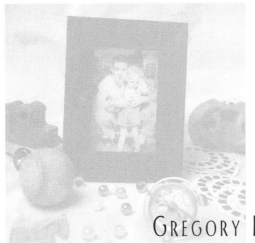

GREGORY E. LANG

WITH PHOTOGRAPHS BY JANET LANKFORD-MORAN

CUMBERLAND HOUSE

AN IMPRINT OF SOURCEBOOKS, INC.®

Published by Cumberland House Publishing, an imprint of Sourcebooks, Inc.
P.O. Box 4410, Naperville, Illinois 60567–4410
(630) 961–3900
Fax: (630) 961–2168
www.sourcebooks.com

Printed and bound in Canada
TR 10 9 8 7 6 5 4 3 2 1

On behalf of my brothers, David, Kevin, and Jody,
and myself, this book is lovingly dedicated to
Jacobs Eugene Lang, our dad.
—GREG

To John, my husband/photo assistant, thank you
for your encouragement and patience.
—JANET

INTRODUCTION

I am the first-born child of a household that included five children before my dad was thirty years old. Ours was the house that never seemed to sleep, with constant activity swirling around it and within it, the one that seemed nearly to burst at the edges as the children who called it home continued to grow. My dad worked hard to provide for his family, but also made time to be with his children, both together and one-on-one. He made sure the tree house we built ourselves was sturdy and safe, that my soapbox racer would indeed cross the finish line, and that once big enough to see over the steering wheel, each child, sitting in his lap, got a chance to drive through the neighborhood in their choice of the station wagon or the old pickup truck.

I have many heartwarming memories from my youth: my dad showing me how to hit a curve ball in the front yard; working with Dad on a Boy Scout project to earn a coveted merit badge; handing him his tools as he tinkered with the car or improved the house on a Sunday afternoon. My dad loved to fish. I remember being awakened by him before sunrise on Saturday mornings, and whispering so as not to awaken my younger siblings, the two of us slipping outside to go fishing. Standing at the water's edge we sometimes talked. Other times we were both content just to listen to the morning sounds. In these early years of my life, my dad was my hero.

As I became a teenager our relationship began to change. Like most young people, I considered myself misunderstood and overtly controlled. I wanted to wear the "in" clothes and stay out late with my friends, shirking my chores and other responsibilities. My demonstrations of rebellion irritated my dad like a pesky splinter under a fingernail. Both being strong willed, my dad and I clashed often. My stormy coming-of-age years were difficult for both of us. At times our disputes were serious enough that I questioned our love for one another, and I wondered what happened to the man who had taught me how to fish. When I left home I promised myself I would not be like him when I became a man, and most certainly not when I became a father.

By the time I entered graduate school my dad and I had come to a peaceful co-existence. We were different, but we could get along. We would not talk much, but we would not argue either. The emotion between us was warm, but not embracing. I could thank him for the money he would slip into my pocket when he thought I wasn't looking and for welcoming me as I came home now and then for one of Mom's soothing Sunday meals. He could tell me he was proud of what I had accomplished. Our relationship was not what it had been, but it was such that I could love him again. This will be okay, I thought to myself. I did not imagine then that years later we would find ourselves sharing a deep bond, that I would feel intensely for him, and that I would be giving my dad credit for helping to shape me into the man I would become.

Today, with more years and a few hundred thousand miles under my feet, I have come to see my father very differently. Now being a father of an emerging teenager and experiencing for myself the stresses and challenges I must have presented in my youth, I smile when I realize my daughter and I are playing out the same debates and negotiations my father and I once did. Now, wiser, I know it was not that I was misunderstood or controlled, but that I lacked the life experience to know what risks I was taking, the judgment to get myself out of trouble before a permanent scar might be made, and the understanding that it *was* possible something bad could happen to me. Today I know my dad was protecting me from what I could not see and simply trying to save himself from the gut-wrenching fear of allowing his child to let go of his hand.

A dad has the responsibility of providing for his family. Sometimes the difficulties of that task go unrecognized and without gratitude. Now having that responsibility for myself—and for only one child, I might add—I look back in *amazement* at what my dad did. He sometimes worked two jobs to support his family; he pushed himself beyond his education to acquire the skills necessary for a better career; and he never bought things for himself before he took care of his children. We ate well, dressed warmly, received gifts, and went on vacations. Even today he continues to extend help to his adult children when he thinks it is needed. I have called him in the middle of the night and he has come to me.

On my mantel, next to a high school portrait of my mom and amid many photographs of my daughter, sits a picture of my dad and me in the front yard of my parents' first house. He is squatting down, his arms wrapped around me as I stand between his knees. Sometimes as I reflect on what is important to me, I stand before this mantel and look at those photographs, realizing how blessed I am to have these loving parents and this wonderful child. As I think of the difficult years of my youth, I think that perhaps I owe my parents, especially my dad, an apology, but know that they would wave me off and accuse me of being silly. I think of things I would like to do for them, and I look forward to each time I hurry my daughter into the car and make a trip to the home I left so many years ago. I am eager to get there, to kiss Mom, and to sit on the front porch and talk with Dad.

Now having come full circle as a son who once worshipped, then disfavored, and now deeply admires his dad, and being a father trying my best to parent but finding myself always second-guessing my abilities, I wonder if my teenage daughter will ever look at me with dancing eyes again. I think the role of being a dad is the greatest challenge and the highest reward a man can have. Reflecting on my dad and me, I know my child and I will have a wonderful, loving, and long-lasting relationship because my dad and I have one. I know that in the end I will be satisfied with my performance as a father because my dad showed me how to do it. And I can believe that I have been a good son because my dad tells me so. I love you, Dad, I do. And I am proud to be your son.

WHY A SON NEEDS A DAD

A son needs a dad

to show him how to shave.

A son needs a dad

who can be playful and silly.

A son needs a dad . . .

to wrestle with him in the grass.

to teach him to be a gracious winner
as well as a gracious loser.

to help him build a tree house.

A son needs a dad . . .

to take him camping.

to teach him how things work.

to teach him how to fix things himself.

A son needs a dad

to show him how to be productive with his hands.

A son needs a dad . . .

to teach him how to talk with girls.

to teach him to apologize for reckless words.

to pull him back when he is headed in the wrong direction.

A son needs a dad

to take him fishing.

A son needs a dad . . .

to listen when others have grown
tired of listening.

to encourage him when he meets with disappointment.

to teach him that it is wise to seek advice.

A son needs a dad

to tell him that he is proud of him.

A son needs a dad . . .

to help him learn from his mistakes.

to talk with about the tough
decisions he will face.

to show him how to control his temper.

to tell him that all is not hopeless,
even when it may seem that it is.

A son needs a dad

to teach him to always give a good day's work.

A son needs a dad . . .

to tell him that there is no disgrace in losing.

to show him how to compromise.

to help him try again after he has stumbled.

A son needs a dad

to go with him on imaginary adventures.

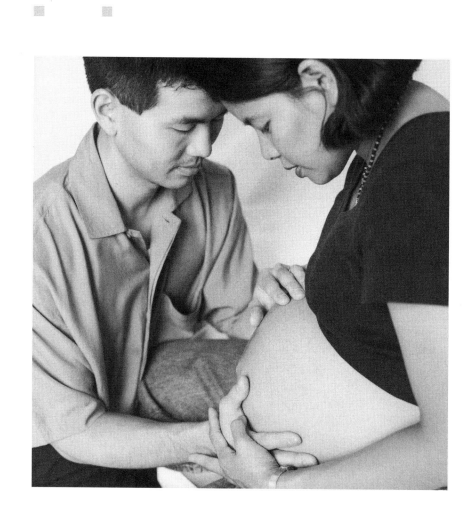

A son needs a dad

to make the family whole.

A son needs a dad

to help him face his challenges with confidence.

A son needs a dad

to be a doting grandfather for his children.

A son needs a dad . . .

who will expect him to play fair.

to take him to baseball games.

so that he will have at least one hero

he can depend on.

A son needs a dad . . .

to teach him to treat women with kindness.

to teach him that men and women are equals.

to stand with him the day he marries.

to show him how to be a good husband.

A son needs a dad

to nurture his independence.

■　　■　　■　　■　　■　　■　　■

A son needs a dad

to teach him that respect must be earned.

A son needs a dad

to prepare him for being responsible
for his own family.

A son needs a dad

who knows how to have fun.

A son needs a dad . . .

who will show him that love is unselfish.

who will not expect the unreasonable from him.

who will discipline him firmly and fairly,
while loving him relentlessly.

who will teach him to avoid selfish temptations.

A son needs a dad

who will be there for him when he needs help.

A son needs a dad

to provide the guidance that will steer him from trouble.

A son needs a dad

who will help him to discover his place in life.

A son needs a dad . . .

to teach him not to use others for his own benefit.

to provide moral guidance as he becomes a man.

to urge him to pursue worthy goals.

to tell him often that he is loved.

A son needs a dad

to help him understand it isn't necessary
to be like everyone else.

A son needs a dad

to teach him when to lead and when to follow.

■   ■   ■   ■   ■   ■   ■

A son needs a dad

to show him unconditional love.

■   ■   ■   ■   ■   ■   ■

A son needs a dad

to show him the difference between
being firm and being stubborn.

A son needs a dad . . .

who will help his mother.

to teach him to be respectful of women.

to teach him how to be a gentleman.

to help him plan for his future.

A son needs a dad

to let him be his equal now and then.

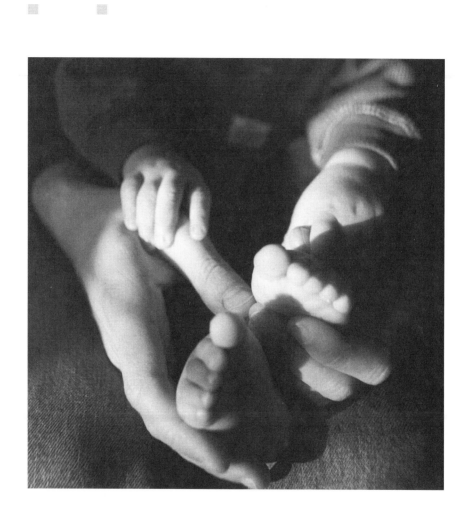

A son needs a dad

to help him find his way.

A son needs a dad

to show him how to tie a necktie.

A son needs a dad

to teach him that family is more important than work.

A son needs a dad

to show him patience.

A son needs a dad

to build a loving house on a foundation
of wisdom and understanding.

A son needs a dad . . .

to teach him to stand up for himself.

to help ease the burdens that
weigh heavily on him.

to tell him that ignorance is not an excuse.

A son needs a dad

to give him the gentle pushes that help him grow.

A son needs a dad

who will protect him when he is not strong
enough to protect himself.

A son needs a dad . . .

to share with him the wisdom he has not yet acquired.

to show him how to love others, even when it is hard.

to teach him to be accountable for his wrongdoings.

A son needs a dad . . .

to teach him that strength is best expressed with restraint.

to lead him toward faith.

to teach him how to maintain dignity in difficult times.

A son needs a dad

to encourage him when he is in doubt of himself.

A son needs a dad

to encourage patriotism and civic responsibility.

A son needs a dad . . .

to teach him to recognize the truth and reward it.

to teach him to recognize sincerity and encourage it.

to teach him to give more than he takes.

to be the standard by which he will

later measure himself.

A son needs a dad

who will give the comfort of protection and affection.

A son needs a dad

who welcomes self-expression.

A son needs a dad . . .

to teach him that he does not always

need to be in control.

to tell him it is okay to admit his mistakes.

to teach him to think about consequences

before he acts.

A son needs a dad

who will show him affection without hesitation.

A son needs a dad

who allows him to question.

A son needs a dad

to teach him to accept the differences in others.

A son needs a dad

who is willing to make sacrifices for his family.

A son needs a dad . . .

to teach him to take pride in providing

for the family.

to teach him to honor the woman who loves him.

to teach him that forgiving is always

the right thing to do.

A son needs a dad

to be the role model for the father he will become.

A son needs a dad

to teach him not to let pride get in the way of listening.

■   ■   ■   ■   ■   ■   ■

A son needs a dad . . .

to comfort him when he cries.

to teach him to be honest at all times.

to show him the meaning of the word *reliable*.

A son needs a dad

because without him he will have less
in his life than he deserves.

To Contact the Author or Photographer

write in care of the publisher:
Cumberland House Publishing/Sourcebooks, Inc.
P.O. Box 4410
Naperville, IL 60567-4410

e-mail the author or visit his Web site:
greg.lang@mindspring.com
www. gregoryelang.com

e-mail the photographer or visit her Web site:
janet@oijoyphoto.com
www.oijoyphoto.com